PRAISE FOR *HEATING THE C*

"These poems live in a bachelor apartment over the corner store. They're on the bus looking out at the muddy hangtime between winter and spring, in a too-warm jacket. These poems will make you a cup of tar-coffee and tell you about the ache of desire in the language of crunching snow. You'll come back to them over and over again to listen."
—Carleigh Baker, author of *Bad Endings*

"Marie-Andrée Gill's spare, luminous micropoems are endlessly surprising, twisting out, into, and unto themselves like complicated lovers. Defiantly fragmentary, these are stunning shards of tongues, embodied vernaculars slowly, steadily unsettling grammars. Kristen Renee Miller's translations retain the elegance and shimmer of the originals while wondrously conveying their knottedness, their syntax of skin. When at last we reach Nitassinan, we are reminded of the worlds poetry documents, but also of the worlds it creates. This is poetry that claims the power to 'gnaw the meat off each day and spit out the pin bones' through a language as unresolved as our decolonial dreams and as necessary as our sovereign desires."
—Urayoán Noel, author of *Transversal*

"Marie-Andrée Gill's *Heating the Outdoors* is a stunning collection exploring heartbreak, and the awkward dance between exes from the positionality of an Ilnu and Québécoise woman whose poetic 'gasoline-soaked heart' yearns deeply for love. Translated by Kristen Renee Miller from French into English, Gill's *Heating the Outdoors* re-wilds the ritualistic humdrum of domestic life while honouring the land and her 'crème-soda ancestral spirit.'"
—Shannon Webb-Campbell, author of *Lunar Tides*
and *I Am a Body of Land*

MARIE-ANDRÉE GILL

Translated by Kristen Renee Miller

Literature in Translation Series

Book*hug Press
Toronto 2023

FIRST ENGLISH EDITION

Originally published as *Chauffer le dehors* © 2019 by Marie-Andrée Gill and
Éditions La Peuplade
Translation © 2023 by Kristen Renee Miller

This edition is published by arrangement with Éditions La Peuplade in conjunction
with its duly appointed agent Books And More Agency #BAM, Paris, France.

Library and Archives Canada Cataloguing in Publication

Title: Heating the outdoors / Marie-Andrée Gill ; translated by Kristen Renee Miller.
Other titles: Chauffer le dehors. English
Names: Gill, Marie-Andrée, author. | Miller, Kristen Renee, translator.
Series: Literature in translation series.
Description: Series statement: Literature in translation series | Poems. | Translation of:
Chauffer le dehors.
Identifiers: Canadiana (print) 20220457859 | Canadiana (ebook) 20220457999
ISBN 9781771668149 (softcover)
ISBN 9781771668163 (PDF)
ISBN 9781771668156 (EPUB)
Classification: LCC PS8613.I439 C5313 2023 | DDC C841/.6—dc23

The production of this book was made possible through the generous assistance of the Canada
Council for the Arts and the Ontario Arts Council. Book*hug Press also acknowledges the
support of the Government of Canada through the Canada Book Fund and the Government
of Ontario through the Ontario Book Publishing Tax Credit and the Ontario Book Fund.

 Canada Council
for the Arts
Conseil des Arts
du Canada

 ONTARIO ARTS COUNCIL
CONSEIL DES ARTS DE L'ONTARIO
an Ontario government agency
un organisme du gouvernement de l'Ontario

 ONTARIO CREATES | ONTARIO CRÉATIF

Funded by the
Government
of Canada

Financé par le
gouvernement
du Canada

 Canada

Book*hug Press acknowledges that the land on which we operate is the traditional territory
of many nations, including the Mississaugas of the Credit, the Anishnabeg, the Chippewa,
the Haudenosaunee, and the Wendat peoples. We recognize the enduring presence of many
diverse First Nations, Inuit, and Métis peoples and are grateful for the opportunity to
meet, work, and learn on this territory.

For Danaé

I don't know if tomorrow will keep me whole
I say the hope of letting yourself be
Holds off despair

—Joséphine Bacon

LIKE NOTHING EVER HAPPENED

The way you blow a kiss
kept in your palm
I blow words
with a stale hope in the pit of my throat
a last drink of milk
before it expires

A caress without purpose, a splicing of limbs, a dust kitten on the floor, a room closed off in fall, a scab torn off, regrown.

I lay my remains on the stove, and my birds hide themselves away to die.

Love is a virgin forest
then a clearcut
in the next line

You're the clump of blackened spruce
that lights my gasoline-soaked heart

It's just impossible you won't be back
to quench yourself in my crème-soda
ancestral spirit

Like nothing ever happened, the lakes keep mass-producing sheep, the people huffing photos, and the machines triggering vertigo and spouting baloney.

Sometimes I close my eyes and pretend I'm there:

You flip the choke, yank the cord, and we take off in a black
cloud. With this much snow, we can't break down; I'm not
even wearing a coverall. I'm enveloped by something like that
saying, *everything in its own place*. You steer through trees in
the dark, turn on a dime. Branches in my face, flakes in my
eyes—with you I'd never get stranded.

It would make a good title for something, I tell myself:
Dances with ski-doos.

Still, I wish we'd poached again, that you'd laced up my fur in your fingerless gloves, that you'd wrung out my heart like mounting a pelt to a frame. I'd have shown you I can smile at myself as a carcass of the word *dread*.

On days when things are just okay, I turn up at le monde,
the world you can enter without knocking.
With my storm damage seeping
through all my concealment, I let loose my call:
have you got beer, mate / have you got beer, mate
if there's no beer, mate / I'm fucking off, mate.

Obviously
I'm not thinking of you
definitely not

Still writing to survive, I make to-do lists, interpret fading images from good dreams: fried onions and hot soups, chanterelles and apple tarts, our accidents of simple happiness.

Even as dreams lose their contours, this practice gleams solid—the materiality of words. I know what to do and not do. I have the manual for these things, the rituals.

Something in me keeps its lamp on—a rip, not a wound but like when clouds break open, between the lungs, an impulse that can't help but look for trouble, pick a fight, try anything that—

I'm still hoping
for a door cracking open
for a daybreak
between the lines of our story

But I admit
I would trade my heart simply
for a good bowl of macaroni
and sausages

It's a love story like all my others
a bus marked *Select*
with nobody on board

*All the changes, even small ones: the flower
arrangement on the table, the new book just
lying there, the frame on a different wall. I
inventory these fixtures of the household—
your home. Each detail nudges me, seizes me,
makes me admit it's been a while. It's the truth
I know already, made more: I'm no longer
part of the decor. To all these things, I'm just a
person passing through.*

*Even now my mark fades: earrings from
beside the mirror, sweater from behind the
door, hair elastic from the floor, one of my
tupperwares from the tupperware drawer.
After our turbulent intimacy, I linger on all
the things over which I have no say: clothes
on the laundry hamper, gourds left on the
sill, a child's new drawing beside the phone,
a completely unknown engagement on the
calendar. They nip at me, the sadnesses of
being here—cut off from little things, written
out of the routine.*

*I never imagined objects, when you look at
them closely, might offer up some truth about
the pleated feelings I'm trying to smooth out.*

Back for my little walkthrough, I lay out what I have to offer as simply as I know how. Maybe this time, who knows, he'll no longer fear everything I stand for.

If you want to know where I am now,
that's me, writing *hey, what's up*
in zamboni meltwater.

SOLFÈGE OF STORMS

From the woods
to the pits I'm seeking
the cure to your sweetness that bites
she who lets me play a role
other than that of bait

Landscapes all look like you when you light them up—
polluted woods and streams, uishkatshan
and hawks that appear when you wish for them,
maples along the coulees, shady folds
of the mountains, a sunset that pricks a line
of conifers and the tshiuetin that slaps the houses,
plates of good food and joyrides—
the seasons no longer hold any meaning
except in the arrangement of our bodies.

I'd like to say all that
and quit biting
the skin from my lips

I feel the struggle of our pulses
each testing the other's patience
but I tell myself whatever happens
the forest will devour me again with its colour
the colour of your eyes

　　At least that's something

In the village we watch each other live; we turn to all the cars that pass; we mark, with orange flags on the edges of dirt roads, all the places we left our beliefs.

I imagine you'll hear me
if I think loud enough
and you'll appear on my threshold

still on the goddamn threshold
there but with a coat on your back

there but not there

I eat it hot whenever I go to the co-op or the pharmacy. There's always a memory loitering down an aisle or a corny love song playing, and it perks me up.

It's like that saying I hate: *eat your hand but keep the other for tomorrow.*

Fear, I keep it for the shining eyes of night animals. I keep it for stories of dead children, for black ice and beetles in my hair.

Fear, it's running into each other at the minimart and not knowing what to do with our bodies.

They go quiet by day
and swell up again at night

I wanted to learn
to read your ebb and flow
and the solfège of your storms

I'm haunted by all the space that I will live without you:
even the effing poems of Brautigan.

Where do I even begin to switch off my hopes, slow down my hamster, become at one with everything that struggles to survive.

*I'm standing on my crushed castle, asking
just five minutes more of reverie, of eating my
heart out. I invent firecrackers beneath our
clothes, conjure us up, call us back to the lip of
pleasure.*

*It's always like this, if I'm honest: passing your
street or your parked car by the hardware
store, I dream up all the ways I might slip
around your neck, knowing very well it goes
nowhere. Logic evaporates, and the only
thought left is of a provocation, of five electric
minutes in which time dilates and dissolves,
a bouquet of smoke, a dandelion parachute
touching down on water.*

*I've been wondering where to live, where
to put my tender parts to broil, if not in
the proxy worlds made by writing, by
reconstructing events, by embellishing
memories which fall silent and reverberate at
the same time. Where to live, if not in those
ecstatic moments and the possibility they'll
come again?*

On a bed of fir saplings, we touched that mute, ephemeral beauty. We stumbled out, uncertain, searching for the edible root of language, nursing our dazzling wounds. Together we drove a street sweeper over our ghosts.

In any case, we knew what to do with our bodies between thunderstorms.

Sometimes I close my eyes and pretend I'm there:
You hold the trout; I pull out the hook. With my thumb in
the gill, I crack the bone and kill it. I'm proud to know how to
do that; I think I'm good.

Christ it sucks to have been so happy.

I'm that face still full of promises
a billboard for the losing candidate
the day after the election

Each detail of your ordinary beauty hurts me.

I make up stories at every turn in the road. Stories I won't tell because I'm sick of tangling my feet in my own head.

How the hell to quit running after you?

*I'm writing to you from my inner infinity pool.
I scream on mute in the quicksand of low-rent
housing, throw salt over my shoulder, turn
back to check a perpetual last time because, as
everyone knows, you can't stop to think when
the carpet catches fire.*

*Everything around me closes and opens. I
want to unlearn the smell of your hair, and
yet—even yet, I tell you—I want to lie on that
mattress in the back of your car, to wake up in
your hands, to be kids again, bursting cherry
tomatoes and chocolates in our mouths, even
though I know that we'll sink into our old
dramas, that we'll prick the bubble, take a
hard fall, and get back on the bike.*

If you're wondering where I am now, that's me, right there, with the forced smile of a figure skater picking herself up after landing a triple axel on her ass.

THE RIOT STARTS WITHIN

My only home
is a punch
in the heart meat

At last we cross paths and we don't hold back. The air fills with the scent of sex bombs reigniting in the skating rink trailers, in the haunts behind our eyes. Your door is closing but it's not shut. It lets me in with the drifting snow, in panties, into your sheets.

We're a glass of water spilled on a keyboard, canned preserves about to burst.

It all comes back; it begins again: the riot starts within.

Kissing: it's just like the movies. You take off slowly, float toward the gym ceiling, get tangled in championship banners from bygone years.

Each breath is a chaos
each smile a survivor, crashed
with geese in its jet engines

I try to reassemble your molecules, to shape
your face with all the winter words I know.
I cry over the dishes, I cry at the parents'
meeting, I cry in my Ricardo biscuits, and
then—shit—cry again as I shovel down the
last of my own powdered crumbs.

At the bottom of my feed, keeping watch for
new messages, I lose myself in the infinity
of the machine: a guy fucks up his tailbone
jumping onto a frozen pool, a cat falls in a
toilet, a little girl swings at a piñata and hits
a man between the legs. Before I know it,
I've scrolled down to the only photos of you
I've taken, blinking like a speak & spell, the
ones of you looking noncommittal in front of
Jonquière mall, and I finally dissolve.

I know I shouldn't do this, but I do it all the
same. And everything hits at once, tidied into
a single disaster on the agenda.

I'm just looking for a sign
to sweep out the ashes
and turn the damper key

Just a sign
for a rent-a-devil
to haul out all your anguish

I carve the birds for supper, as I would do to you but in reverse: graft onto you articulated wings and full-throated cries, so you could see the savage flowers of my raw heart, the thousand-year medicine that envelops us.

It's so corny
I must have hauled out thirty loads of laundry
I just can't part
with your fingerprints

When my ears ring or I drop a utensil, I force myself not to check for a car pulling up in the yard.

Each thought a crash
of jackdaws in a blender
a brand-new subject to drop in

All those Céline tunes
I sing in my car
quench my sugar rages
for you

What remains:
crying laughing like everyone knows
the scent of laundry soap and two-stroke gasoline
and my clit like a ronde dancer
all alone when her turn comes

I tempt myself to the edge of a fjord, to a secret place with no paths. A seal appears beside me, dancing in the water. I shout HELLO BABY, *and he startles and swims off.*

In the night, no wind. I wake to the quiet breaths of belugas, a new lullaby, a medley of hugeness and grace. And this is what it feels like exactly: a sparkling gratitude, the words thank you flashing neon above my hair.

I awake to mist, thick mist filled with sunlight—the blurred, radiant expanse, the fluid sweetness, the subtle voice of the air. I want to take the mist for what it is, though I can't help but see a moving, surreal, pointillist painting—a gift.

I touch myself, I read, a squirrel scrambles over me—I'm a Disney fucking princess. I tramp through the dense forest; I scratch myself everywhere and I like it. This body, haunted by backcountry, bears marks of pride and autonomy, endurance and strength. In these moments I'm all here, unkillable— nothing much and everything all at once.

And this pulls me out of my head. The closer I get to nature, the more I feel worthy of its voice, of mine.

Outside is the only answer I found inside.

THE FUTURE SHRUGS

I make these poems
the way you make firewood

—Antoine Dumas

We've played doctor long enough
upon each of our multicoloured bruises

I, too, can run after elk and listen to the uncomplicated poetry of aspen.

Under the snow-drunk sun I replace you, in each new trail I open and enter like a woman in heat, in the sharp, bright paths of snowflakes, being born.

I want to keep a little crooked
what remains of sweetness:
spells blown hot into the holes of our fists
felted boot liners beside the stove
a rubbed balloon left stuck to the wall

You know when you dig a snow tunnel à deux, each taking a side, the moment the shovels touch and the centre falls open and the walls expand outward: that's us; that, I know.

With respect
to all our attempts
I won't end up in an asylum
of my accumulating empties

With the word *slowly* as an ally, I connect the dots in
ascending order, make myself a new face; I sweep up the
sawdust; I gnaw the meat off each day and spit out the pin
bones.

How to put it differently:
we're brimming
with colours
only visible
when we close our eyes

Roused by dreams of seeking my place somewhere out on the trail, I put on my pretty dress to sing pop songs among the deer, to peel bark from whatever comes next.

Even if the future shrugs its shoulders and untangles its threads quietly but not quickly, I know we will disappear to someplace other than the sky, the sky we've unzipped just wide enough to inhabit.

I let the territory scatter me like the migratory birds that don't know how to lose their way.

What keeps us from submerging is the light that draws us toward shelter. Miracles always come back when you learn the words again.

It's enough to make me disarrange the furniture, let out the cat, and lie down in wait for the mountain, taking its slow walk across the millennia, even as blowflies blossom at last from my belly.

I want to feel that freedom
of driving after dark
in some unknown town
so late the red lights are flashing

I touch wood; I close my mouth, but I keep on repeating
to the encompassing silence:

if you are looking for me, I am home
or somewhere on Nitassinan;
all my doors and windows are open.

I'm heating the outdoors.

It's in the sacré of a sunrise
in the music of our surviving animals
in the sorrow of all that shines

in all the slowness
my shaky breath allows

I let time
tune its instrument
accordingly

NOTES

Some of these poems appeared in other versions in the original French in the publications *Au Village*, with Éditions OQP, and *Le cœur-réflexe*, at Possibles Éditions.

"On days when things are just okay ..." includes lines from the song "Y'a tu d'la bière icitte" by Famille Soucy.

"Landscapes all look like you ..." opens with a line from the album *D'eux* by Céline Dion and Jean-Jacques Goldman. I admit that I restrained myself from adding more.

"I'm haunted by all the space ..." opens with lines from *The Pill vs. the Springhill Mine Disaster* by Richard Brautigan.

The guy who fucks up his tailbone jumping onto a frozen pool is here: https://www.youtube.com/watch?v=QGvId8r7Jhs

And finally, *uishkatshan* is a gray jay; *tshiuetin* is the north wind; and *Nitassinan* is Our Land. These are Ilnu-aimun words.

ACKNOWLEDGEMENTS

From the author:

Thanks to Roseline for the open, challenging discussions and the poetic guidance; to Ève for your attentiveness, your gentleness, and your commentary; to Guylaine for your invaluable presence and sensitivity; to Jo Lamy and Jo Gill for your read-throughs; to Gaëlle Étémé, Véro Gauthier, Laurance, Julie-Van, Evelyne, and Mom. You don't know it, but your listening and your words at certain moments really did me good, made me see things from new angles.

Thank you, Paul and Mylène; it's not complicated, working with you is precious. Thank you, Simon; you're the one who convinced me to get into this. And thank you to Marc-Antoine.

Thank you, Kristen, for translating my work, and Jay and Hazel of Book*hug Press for publishing it in English.

Thanks to Hayden, Aleksi, and Milo, because I think you'll be happy (or not) to see your names here, but especially for your cuddles and your nonsense every day.

Thank you, Danaé, for your crazy sincerity, which mirrors my own, for the love that has enlarged us, and for the poem about the red lights flashing.

From the translator:

All my thanks to Hazel and Jay at Book*hug Press; to Urayoán Noel, who chose a selection of this work for the Gulf Coast Prize in Translation; to the editors at *Gulf Coast*, *jubilat*, *The Arkansas International*, and *Denver Quarterly*, who published select translations; and to the Third Coast Translators Collective, for your read-throughs, encouragement, and camaraderie.

And my thanks to the National Endowment for the Arts, the American Literary Translators Association, the Kentucky Foundation for Women, and Hermitage Artist Retreat, whose support helped make this work in translation possible.

ABOUT THE AUTHOR

PHOTO: SOPHIE GAGNON-BERGERON

Ilnu Nation member Marie-Andrée Gill grew up on the Mashteuiatsh reserve in the Saguenay-Lac-Saint-Jean region in Quebec, home to the Pekuakamiulnuatsh community. She is the acclaimed author of three French-language poetry collections from La Peuplade: *Béante*, *Frayer*, and *Chauffer le dehors*. Two of her books have been translated into English by Kristen Renee Miller, including *Spawn* (2020) and *Heating the Outdoors* (2023). A doctoral student in literature, Gill's research and creative work focus on the decolonial project of writing the intimate. She hosts the award-winning Radio-Canada podcast "Laissez-nous raconter: L'histoire crochie" ("Telling Our Twisted Histories"), which "reclaims Indigenous history by exploring words whose meanings have been twisted by centuries of colonization." Gill's work has been nominated for many awards, including the

Governor General's Literary Award for Poetry, and she is a three-time recipient of the Salon du Livre Prize in Poetry. She has also won two Indigenous Voices Awards, including the Best Published Poetry in French prize for *Chauffer le dehors*. Also in 2020, Gill was named Artist of the Year by the Quebec Council of Arts and Letters.

ABOUT THE TRANSLATOR

Kristen Renee Miller is the executive director and editor-in-chief for Sarabande Books. A poet and translator, she is a 2023 NEA Fellow and the translator of two books from the French by poet Marie-Andrée Gill: *Spawn* (2020) and *Heating the Outdoors* (2023). Her work can be found widely, including in *POETRY*, *The Kenyon Review*, and *Best New Poets*. She is the recipient of fellowships and awards from the Foundation for Contemporary Arts, AIGA, the John F. Kennedy Center for the Performing Arts, the Gulf Coast Prize in Translation, and the American Literary Translators Association. She lives in Louisville, Kentucky.

COLOPHON

Manufactured as the first English edition of
Heating the Outdoors
in the spring of 2023 by Book*hug Press

Copy edited by Andrea Waters
Proofread by Rachel Gerry
Type + design by Tree Abraham

Printed in Canada

bookhugpress.ca